D1509319

ABOUT
THE HUMAN BODY

PUBLISHER	Joseph R. DeVarennes
PUBLICATION DIRECTOR	Kenneth H. Pearson
ADVISORS	Roger Aubin
	Robert Furlonger
EDITORIAL SUPERVISOR	Jocelyn Smyth
PRODUCTION MANAGER	Ernest Homewood
PRODUCTION ASSISTANTS	Martine Gingras — Kathy Kishimoto
	Catherine Gordon — Peter Thomlison
CONTRIBUTORS	Alison Dickie — Nancy Prasad
	Bill Ivy — Lois Rock
	Jacqueline Kendel — Merebeth Switzer
	Anne Langdon — Dave Taylor
	Sheila Macdonald — Alison Tharen
	Susan Marshall — Donna Thomson
	Pamela Martin — Pam Young
	Colin McCance
SENIOR EDITOR	Robin Rivers
EDITORS	Brian Cross — Ann Martin
	Anne Louise Mahoney — Mayta Tannenbaum
PUBLICATION ADMINISTRATOR	Anna Good
ART AND DESIGN	Richard Comely — Ronald Migliore
	Robert B. Curry — Penelope Moir
	George Elliott — Marion Stuck
	Marilyn James — Bill Suddick
	Robert Johanssen — Sue Wilkinson

Canadian Cataloguing in Publication Data

Main entry under title:

Questions kids ask about the human body

(Questions kids ask ; 19)
ISBN 0-7172-2258-5

1. Body, Human—Miscellanea—Juvenile literature.
2. Human physiology—Miscellanea—Juvenile literature.
3. Children's questions and answers.
I. Smyth, Jocelyn.   II. Comely, Richard.   III. Series.

QP37.Q48 1988   j612   C89-093169-2

Questions Kids Ask . . . about THE HUMAN BODY

continued

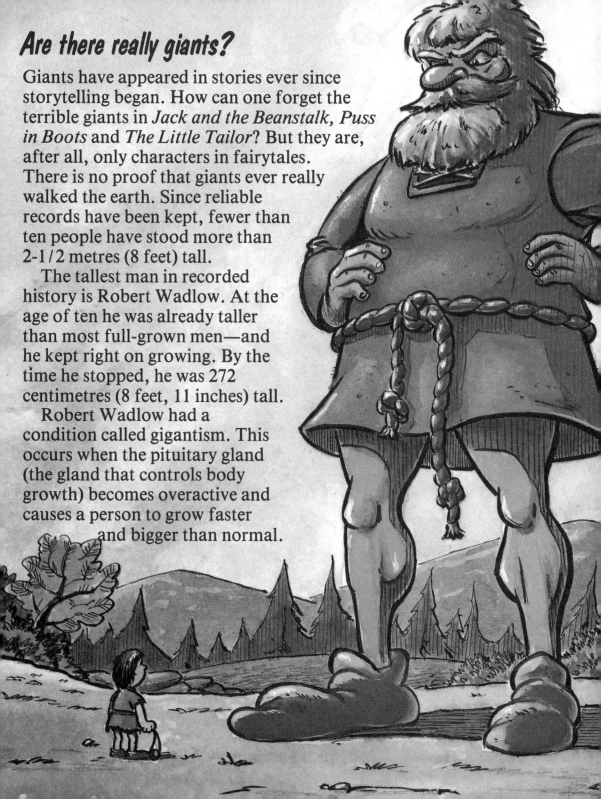

Are there really giants?

Giants have appeared in stories ever since storytelling began. How can one forget the terrible giants in *Jack and the Beanstalk, Puss in Boots* and *The Little Tailor*? But they are, after all, only characters in fairytales. There is no proof that giants ever really walked the earth. Since reliable records have been kept, fewer than ten people have stood more than 2-1/2 metres (8 feet) tall.

The tallest man in recorded history is Robert Wadlow. At the age of ten he was already taller than most full-grown men—and he kept right on growing. By the time he stopped, he was 272 centimetres (8 feet, 11 inches) tall.

Robert Wadlow had a condition called gigantism. This occurs when the pituitary gland (the gland that controls body growth) becomes overactive and causes a person to grow faster and bigger than normal.

What holds our teeth in?

Baby teeth don't have any roots —that is why they fall out so easily when the time comes. But your second set of teeth, the permanent ones, do have roots. They look a bit like long fangs sticking down below the gums, and are actually glued into a socket in the jawbone.

A tough membrane between the root of the tooth and the jaw socket contains special cells. These cells produce a cement that glues the membrane to the tooth on one side and to the jawbone on the other. If people become very sick with certain illnesses, or if they go too long without food, this membrane weakens and shrinks, and teeth can begin to loosen and fall out.

Why do bones break?

Try to touch your left elbow with your left hand. Can you do it? No—because bones don't bend. Our body bends in places because our bones are connected by hinges, or joints, but the individual bones cannot.

When you are very young, your bones are still somewhat spongy and flexible—even if you fall, they will probably not break. As you get older, minerals such as calcium build up in your bones, making them harder and more likely to break than bend under stress.

What is a bruise?

Ouch! Someone punches you in the arm. Or you bump into the sharp corner of a table. The next day you have a purple bruise. Why is it purple?

A hard blow smashes thousands of tiny blood vessels under the top layer of your skin. Blood trickles in among these skin cells where it doesn't belong. The red blood cells die and fall apart, spilling out hemoglobin—the pigment that colors blood red. This makes your bruise purple.

Later on, your bruise turns green and yellow as other chemicals in the dying blood cells are broken down and released.

Gradually, these are absorbed into the blood, and in a short time your bruise is gone.

Why do cuts form scabs?

No matter how careful you are, you've probably scraped or cut your skin at one time. Your body is prepared for little accidents, and gets to work immediately.

Just seconds after you cut yourself, substances in your blood called *platelets* stick to the walls of the cut blood vessel. Gradually they bunch together, narrowing the opening of the broken vessel. This slows the bleeding.

Eventually the platelets seal the opening completely, and the bleeding stops. While they're doing this, they release chemicals that react with other substances in your blood to make sticky strands of *fibrin*. These threads form a ''net'' that catches and holds the blood cells, forming a solid plug, or clot. When the clot is exposed to air, it dries into a hard crust, or scab.

The scab protects the open cut so new skin tissue can grow. When the new tissue is healthy and strong, the scab's job is done. It dries up completely and falls off, leaving a new layer of skin underneath.

How many times a minute does your heart beat?

The smaller an animal is, the faster its heart beats. The heart of a canary averages 1000 beats per minute, while an elephant's heart only beats about 25 times a minute. With human beings, it's much the same: a newborn baby's heart beats about twice as fast as an adult's. For a newborn, 130 beats a minute or even more is about normal, while for an adult at rest the number is between 60 and 80. What's yours? Take your pulse and see.

DID YOU KNOW . . . your heart begins to beat even before you are born.

What happens if you get frostbite?

Have you ever been out on a cold winter day and felt a tingling
or numbness in your hands or ears? These are the first signs
of frostbite. You can rub the tingling parts to warm
them or go inside to get heavier clothes. Warming
up will bring you back to normal.

But what if you're having a
good time skating or tobogganing
and you ignore these warning
signs? If you do, your skin will
start to look unnaturally white.
Because you're cold, the blood
moves slowly, making it harder to
reach the outer parts of your
body such as your nose, ears,
hands and feet. And if there's not
enough blood to keep an area
warm, it starts to freeze.

Frostbite, like burns, comes in
three degrees. In second-degree
frostbite, the skin gets very red
and swells up. In third-degree
frostbite, the skin is white and
hard all the way through. When
you warm it, the skin blisters and
the frostbitten tissue drops off.
People have even been known to
lose toes!

So that's why your parents
make such a big fuss about
dressing warmly on cold winter
days and calling you in from time
to time to get warmed up. They
don't want you to get frostbite.

What causes butterflies in your stomach?

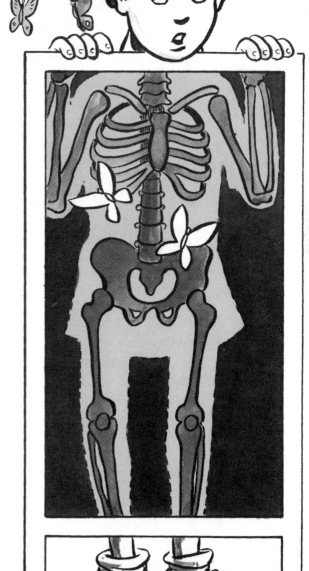

You have to give a speech to the class and you're scared. You stand there, pale and sweating, wishing you were somewhere else. You've forgotten what you want to say. Your heart thumps loudly, your breath comes faster, and it feels as though a bunch of butterflies are fluttering around in your stomach.

That feeling is part of your body's reaction to a scary situation. Your nervous system is sending messages to your glands, which start pouring the hormone adrenalin into your bloodstream. Adrenalin speeds everything up so that you are ready to take ACTION.

So you give your talk. And as soon as the frightening situation is over, your body goes back to normal—and the butterflies fly away.

What is an albino?

A very few people are born with no pigment, or color, in their skin. They are called albinos (from the Latin word for white) because they have milky-white skin and white hair. And while other people have brown, blue or green eyes, an albino's eyes are always pink—the color of the blood vessels in the eye.

Albinos have to be careful about going out in the sun. Since they have no protective pigment, they sunburn very easily.

How long does it take to digest a meal?

You do more work when you eat a meal than you might think. As soon as you begin eating, your body goes right to work so that you get the most out of your food.

The process actually begins in your mouth. Teeth make sure the food that reaches your stomach is properly ground. Saliva helps to soften food and move it down the throat easily.

Once in your stomach, your meal is broken down even further by very strong juices. This chemical process leaves a substance called *chyme*.

Chyme goes from your stomach into the small intestine where the nutrients are absorbed into the bloodstream. What remains then passes into your large intestine and is eliminated as waste.

It usually takes two days for a meal to leave the system entirely. This digestion process happens every time you eat—while you are busy thinking about other things.

Why don't people have tails?

You don't need a tail like a cat's or a squirrel's, but you do have a tail —sort of. It is an extension of your backbone, like a dog's or squirrel's tail is, but it's only one bone long. Feel at the very bottom of your back. The pointed, triangular bone that you feel is your tail. It is called the *coccyx* (sounds like kok-siks). It's not much as tails go— but it's all you have!

Can everyone be hypnotized?

Never mind what you see in the movies. In real life, you can't be hypnotized if you don't want to be. An expert can put you into a trance—like a deep sleep—only if you are willing to follow the hypnotist's suggestions. And it doesn't always work, even when you are willing.

Why would anyone want to be hypnotized? To stop bad habits, such as smoking. Or to overcome

DID YOU KNOW . . . some people can even hypnotize themselves!

fears, such as the fear of crowds. After putting you in a trance, a trained hypnotist suggests ways for you to solve problems when you wake up.

Doctors and dentists are beginning to use hypnosis, especially with people who have bad reactions to anesthetic. That means your dentist could put you into a trance, and pull your tooth—without you feeling much, or any, pain.

14

What is sunstroke?

Have you ever noticed that people living in hot places often wear hats? This is one of the ways they prevent sunstroke.

Sunstroke comes from being out in the very hot sun for so long that the body's usual ways of keeping its temperature normal stop working. When this happens, perspiration stops and body temperature rises rapidly. The skin feels very hot and dry and the pulse beats quickly.

The most important step in case of sunstroke is to cool down —by taking a cold bath, or putting ice packs on the head and neck. Best of all is not to get it, and wearing a hat when you go out in the sun will help.

Why do we breathe?

Take a deep breath. Can you feel your chest expand as air rushes into the air sacs in your lungs? These air sacs are covered with tiny blood vessels. Oxygen enters them and is absorbed into your bloodstream. When the blood leaves your lungs, it carries a fresh supply of oxygen to all your cells. In the cells, the oxygen combines with chemicals from the food you've eaten to produce the energy your cells need.

Just as all living cells need oxygen in order to keep working, they all produce carbon dioxide.

Carbon dioxide is a waste product made when the oxygen and food chemicals combine.

As your blood carries oxygen to your cells, it picks up carbon dioxide and carries it back to your lungs. Your lungs push the carbon dioxide out of your body when you breathe out. And all of this happens every time you take a breath!

Why is blood red?

The answer is one word: hemoglobin. Hemoglobin is the chemical in your red blood cells that makes your blood red.

When your blood travels through your lungs, the hemoglobin combines with the oxygen that you breathe in. Then your blood carries oxygen through your arteries to other parts of your body. This blood is bright red.

The blood in your veins, on the other hand, looks bluish—check the inside of your wrist. This blood is traveling back to your heart to be pumped into your lungs again. Its real color is actually dark red. It looks bluish because you are seeing it through several layers of skin.

DID YOU KNOW . . . blue blood is a term used to describe royalty or nobility. It comes from an observation made long ago in Spain that the nobility appeared to have bluer blood because they had such pale skin.

17

Why do you catch cold?

Ahchoo! If you've been sneezing and have a runny nose and sore throat, chances are you have a cold. How did you catch it?

The cold is a common disease caused by viruses. Cold viruses are usually spread through the sneezes or coughs of a person who already has a cold. There are nearly one hundred different viruses that can cause a cold, and the virus can pass quickly from one person to another.

There is no cure for colds. Medicines may give you some relief from the watery eyes, runny nose, and sore throat that go with a cold, but they won't cure you. The best thing to do is snuggle up in bed and get plenty of rest. Your body will take over from there, and kill the cold virus that caused the infection.

DID YOU KNOW. . . instead of saying "to catch a cold" in some languages people say "to *eat* a cold."

18

Why do you call your little finger a pinkie?

Have you ever wondered why your little finger is called a pinkie? It's no more pink than any of your other fingers.

The word *pinkie* has been around for a very long time. Actually, it started out as *pinkje*, a Dutch word. This word had several meanings, including "a small creature such as an elf," "a young bullock," and—the one we are looking for—"the little finger." The root of all these meanings was an older sense of the word which meant "something small."

What's so special about your thumb?

Most animals' fingers all point in the same direction, but people, monkeys and other primates have thumbs. Your thumb can move through a range of positions up to a 90 degree angle from your hand. This is what it means to have an opposable thumb.

Bend your thumb across the palm of your hand so you can't use it and try to pick something up. Now try it using your thumb. That's better. Your thumb also helps you grip things tightly, and you can also use it to give the thumbs up sign to show that everything is all right. Aren't you glad you have opposable thumbs?

What is a wart?

People used to think that touching toads caused warts, but we now know that they are caused by a virus. The virus makes cells in the top layer of skin multiply and push each other up, forming a tough little bump—a wart.

Folk remedies for getting rid of warts range from reciting magic words to rubbing them with a penny. Strangely enough, it sometimes works.

Scientists say that our attitudes affect our immune system—the body's defense against invading germs. Believing your warts will disappear may give your immune system enough of a boost to help it get the wart virus under control.

How many bones do we have?

At birth babies have about 275 bones in their bodies. As we grow older, though, some of these smaller bones fuse—or grow together—so that by the time we reach adulthood, we have 206 bones.

Bones range in size from the powerful thigh bone—about 51 centimetres (20 inches) long—to the *pisiform,* a bone that lies at the base of the little finger and is the size and shape of a split pea. Some bones are loosely connected—the shoulders, elbows and knees, for example. Other bones, like the pelvis and skull, are sealed together to protect the organs inside.

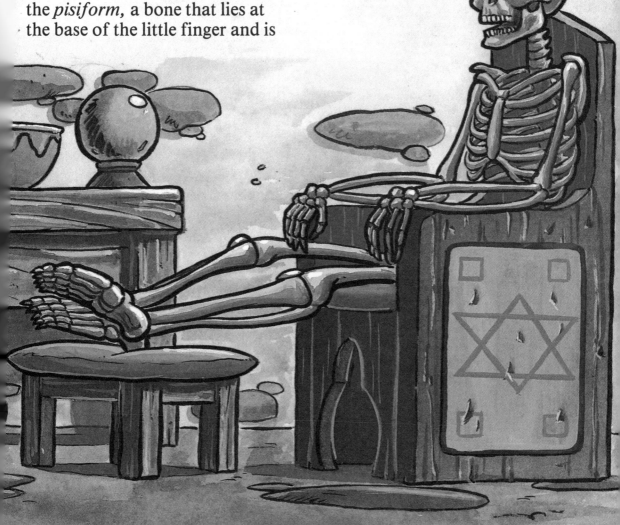

Why do we get itchy?

Itching is a mild form of pain that results when nerve-endings in the skin are stimulated by certain substances. Insect bites and plants like poison ivy make almost everyone itch. Allergies can produce itchy rashes as can illnesses like chicken pox. And many individuals find that a particular cloth or soap makes them itch.

Scratching provides some relief from an itch, but it can make matters worse—as in the case of poison ivy, which spreads when scratched.

What is a reflex action?

A reflex is a body movement that you don't control. All animals have two kinds of reflexes: those they are born with and those they learn.

We are born with many different reflexes. For example, the pupils of your eyes close automatically when a light is shone at them. Reflexes like this organize our very complex bodies and make their different systems work together. If you had to think about adjusting the pupils of your eyes every time the lighting changed, you would never be able to keep up.

The other kind of reflex is the kind we learn. This is sometimes called a conditioned reflex, because it can result from the conditions people live under. The great Russian psychologist Ivan Pavlov investigated this kind of reflex. He discovered that he could train dogs to develop reflex reactions to a command he gave them. First he rang a bell and then he gave the dogs food. After repeating this several times he found the dogs' mouths would water as soon as they heard the bell ring—even if there was no food in sight.

Why do we get thirsty?

Our bodies are like active bank accounts: deposits and withdrawals are being made all the time. When we eat and drink, water is taken in. When we perspire or go to the washroom, water leaves our systems.

A very delicate mechanism in our bodies, called homeostasis, keeps track of our physical accounts. For example, if there's too little water in our systems, the thirst center in our brains is triggered and we begin to feel thirsty. The reason that we are more thirsty on hot days is that our bodies are working overtime to cool us down by perspiring.

DID YOU KNOW . . . the human body is made up of 68 percent water.

LIQUID ASSETS

Why do some men go bald?

A healthy scalp continually sheds old hairs and grows new hairs to replace them. Baldness develops when new hair stops growing in. The most common type of baldness is male-pattern baldness, where a man loses much or all of the hair over the top of his head. This may begin during the teenage years but usually starts somewhat later. Hair loss may be slow or rapid and it can't be prevented or cured.

Male-pattern baldness is inherited. If a man's father goes bald, then he can expect to too. But he can also inherit baldness from his mother if she carries the gene for baldness. She can pass this gene on to her son even though she doesn't lose her own hair.

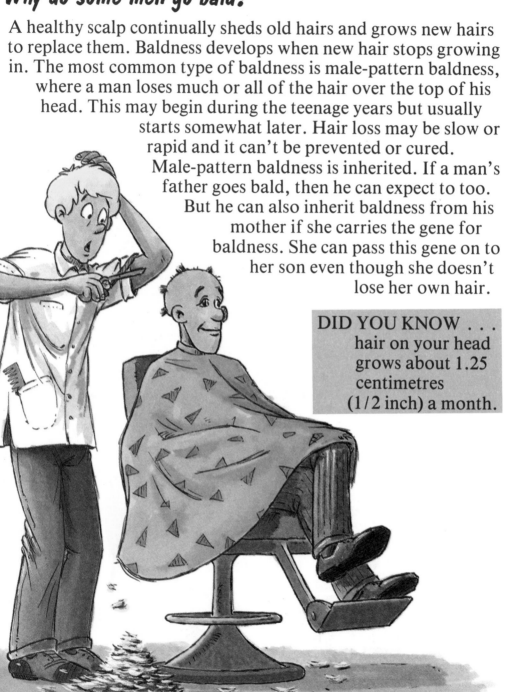

DID YOU KNOW . . . hair on your head grows about 1.25 centimetres (1/2 inch) a month.

Why does hair turn gray?

Your hair is made up of cells. Some of the cells contain pigment (coloring matter), which gives your hair its color. When these cells lose their ability to make pigment, the hairs become colorless, or gray. Most of the time, this doesn't happen until people are older, but sometimes a young person's hair can turn gray too.

Loss of hair pigment may be hereditary, which means you inherit it from your parents. Doctors believe it could also be related to the nervous system. People suffering a lot of mental strain or shock sometimes get white or gray hair quite quickly.

Many people dye their hair to hide the white and gray, but some prefer to let nature take its course. White and gray hair can be very attractive. After all, Santa Claus just wouldn't look like Santa Claus without his snowy white hair and beard!

Why do we have eyebrows?

Your eyes are very important, so your body protects them in special ways. One way is the bony ridge under your eyebrows. It sticks out over your eyes and can keep them from being hit directly if you are struck.

Do eyebrows also protect your eyes? Some people think so. They say our eyebrows prevent sweat and other materials from sliding down our foreheads and into our eyes. Other people say that all eyebrows help us to do is communicate with one another. Go look in the mirror. Make an angry face and then a happy face. Did you see how your eyebrows move?

No one really knows for certain why we have eyebrows. Ask your friends and see what interesting answers they can come up with.

What is the pupil of the eye?

Look in the mirror and you'll see a round black spot in the center of your eye. That's your pupil— an opening to let light enter your eye so you can see. It grows larger or smaller, depending on how much light there is around you.

If it is dark, your pupil grows bigger so that more light can enter. In bright sunlight, your pupil grows smaller. This prevents too much light from getting in and hurting your eyes.

Most cameras have to be adjusted so the right amount of light comes in. But lucky you! Your pupils adjust perfectly all by themselves.

Why do you yawn?

Yawning is an involuntary reflex, which means you do it without thinking about it. You usually yawn when you are tired and your body isn't working as efficiently as usual. Your brain feels it isn't getting enough oxygen, so it triggers the yawning reflex. In comes a big gulp of air to provide the oxygen your brain needs. If you keep on yawning, your body is telling you it's time for bed.

This doesn't explain why you will often yawn if someone else does. Nobody knows for sure why yawns are catchy—so catchy in fact that even reading about them can make you feel so-o-o sleepy . . . z z z z z z

How much of your life is spent sleeping?

One third of your life is spent sleeping. This means that by the time you are 60 years old, you will have spent 20 years asleep!

That may sound like a lot of time, but sleep is very important. We all need sleep to keep our bodies and minds working properly. Without sleep, people become quick-tempered and unable to concentrate, easily distracted, and they make mistakes at even simple tasks.

Why do you shiver?

Human beings are warm-blooded creatures. This means that we are able to regulate the temperature of our bodies. Except when we are sick, our body temperature stays at about 37°C (98.6°F).

DID YOU KNOW . . . babies are unable to shiver until they are about two years old. That is one reason why babies must be kept especially warm.

If you are sick or not wearing enough warm clothes, it is possible for your body temperature to drop below 37°C (98.6°F), and if this happens, then you start to shiver.

Shivering is one of your body's ways of defending itself against cold. When you shiver your muscles contract and expand rapidly. This generates heat and helps keep your body from getting even colder. Shivering is your body's way of telling you to put on more clothes, or to move indoors to a warmer spot if you have been playing outside in the cold for a long time.

When people stop growing do they begin to shrink?

All living things grow. Most healthy human beings stop growing some time between the ages of 18 and 30. After people stop growing in height, they actually begin to shrink. You don't notice it at first because the process is very, very slow (1.2 cm, or half an inch, every 20 years). It usually doesn't become noticeable until a person reaches old age.

The decrease in height happens because pads of cartilage between the bones of the backbone gradually thin out. Eventually, as the cartilage pads thin, the backbone often begins to bend. This is why some elderly people appear to look bent as well as shorter than they used to be.

What are wrinkles?

Have you ever wondered why a baby's skin is smooth, while the skin of older people has deep lines and creases?

Your skin is made up of several layers. One layer contains thin, criss-crossing fibers that stretch and snap back—like elastic. You can frown or wrinkle your forehead, and when you stop, your skin smooths out again.

But as you get older, your skin becomes less elastic and doesn't snap back as easily. Little wrinkles start to form, especially where you repeat the same expression. If you are a frowner, deep lines appear between your eyebrows. Laugh lines or crinkles form around your mouth and eyes.

Anything that dries out your skin, such as overexposure to wind and sun, will speed up the wrinkling process.

Are people getting taller?

Yes and no. Scientists don't think that tall people today are any taller than tall people in the past. But it does seem that today more people are growing to those heights.

There are two reasons why people grow tall. One is heredity —their family history. If your parents and grandparents are tall, there's a good chance you will be too. Different families produce different sizes of people, and scientists don't think the range of heights is changing.

The other reason for tallness is what you eat and how healthy you are. Someone may have the right heredity to grow tall, but if there is never enough food when that person is growing, he or she won't reach that height.

We now know a great deal more about nutrition than people used to. For that and other reasons, more people today eat better and are healthier than in past centuries. Therefore it is possible that more of us are growing to our full heights.

Index _____